Here's what people are saying about **HEY HON!**

"...a laugh-out-loud dictionary of translations that read like conversations overheard at the Patterson Bowling Lanes (**Ahreddy:** as in **Dat sem pin shudda falled ober ahreddy.**)...the most definitive collection of Bawlmerese since John Goodspeed was penning his 'Mr. Peep's Diary' for *The Evening Sun* more than 30 years ago." —- Michael Olesker, *The Baltimore Sun*

"Ah doan talk lake dat!" —- Lorraine, Canton

"Your rendition of the dialect is very accurate. You have a fine ear for the dialect, which is rare among natives of Baltimore, I think. In fact, I guess, natives of almost anywhere rarely hear themselves speaking their dialect as others hear them." —- John Goodspeed ("Mr. Peep")

"Dat is too hal yew talk!" —- Jimmy, Highlandtown

"Various essays and lexicographies have been composed on Bawlmerese before, but never on the scale of **HEY HON!** nor with Mr. Smith's keen ear or exquisite mock-seriousness. Not only Balto-philes but lovers and scholars of the American language will find this book a source of enlightenment ("What <u>was</u> that plumber talking about?") and pleasure." —- Tom Chalkley, Senior Writer, *The City Paper*

"Over a backyard fence, down the alley, and `round the corner to endless rows of white marble steps and ... Bawlmer ... the only town that could ever talk like this. You have created a delightful linguistic jaunt down memory lane; a written preserve for an endangered national treasure so uniquely ours." —- Ron Mullen, Deputy Commissioner, Baltimore City Police (retired)

"...you really captured the unique language spoken in certain segments of our City. At least when people read your manuscript they will know that we in Baltimore are not putting them on, but that many of us actually speak that way - and we are proud of it." —- Kurt Schmoke, Mayor of Baltimore

 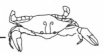

HEY HON!

How to Talk Like a Real Bawlamoron

by Ernest Smith

38th STREET
PRESS

Baltimore

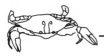 

THANKS

to Fred and Irene, Ern and Marge, June and Bill, Uncle Buzz and Aunt Till, the Smiths, Doushas, Taylors, Rubys, Birxes, Careys, Mundys, D'Antonis, Browns, and Bowersoxes, Owen, Peggy, Edith, Buddy, Lorraine, Walter, Eloise, and John Goodspeed (Mister Peep).

—- E.S.

ACKNOWLEDGEMENTS

"Owen fixin ta gao aout inna snao" reprinted by kind permission of *The Pearl*.
"Baltimore Colts' Fight Song" courtesy of The Baltimore Colts' Band, Inc. John Zieman, President.
All other song lyrics are in the public domain.

Design and production by Robin Raindrop (*Baltimore Resources Journal*)

ISBN 0-9637223-0-1

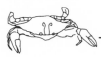 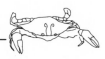

HEY HON!

WELCOME
TO
BAWLMER

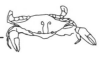

Contents

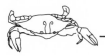 

Introduction

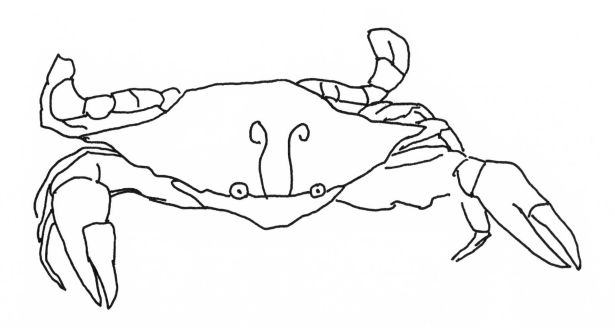

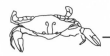

"We may not always say it right, but this is a town where even if you don't know what we're saying you know what we mean." - Russell H., Bawlmer native and seafood wholesaler.

Father to Son

I come from blue collar Baltimore. My father grew up in Pigtown. He worked as a shipfitter and a printer. His father retired from Sparrows Point after thirty years of driving rivets in the car shop. I was born in Waverly and attended P.S. 51, right across the street from Memorial Stadium. As I grew up I learned to talk like a real Bawlamoron, just like all the people around me.

Today there don't seem to be as many Bawlamorons around as there used to be. In the old days, when the kids grew up they moved down the block. Today they move to the suburbs. There, the unique sounds of Bawlmerese are under assault from the forces of assimilation and television. Instead of talking like their neighbors, folks now talk like the people they hear on TV. If you go to certain neighborhoods you can still hear the "*buoys*" talking about "*de O's*" and "*urshters*" and "*lemoran pah*," but you have to listen a little harder.

I have two sons of my own now. With real Bawlamorons seemingly harder to come by, I was worried for a while that they might miss out on the pleasures of Bawlmerese, but once they started to call their mother "*Hon*," I relaxed. They might still need a few pointers, but genes, grandparents, and this guide book should take care of that.

The language I grew up with wouldn't have been the same without the contributions of the black community, but it's still mostly white folks who speak the Bawlmerese decribed in this book. Of course there are lots of words like *ax*, *pixture*, and *poh-leece* which cross all ethnic and racial lines.

Don't expect to hear Bawlmerese in every part of town. Even where you do find it there will be variations. Each neighborhood is like a separate tribe, speaking its own version of the mother tongue and proud of its individuality. I hope this book manages to capture some of the sounds and spirit of the tribes of Bawlmer, my hometown.

The Origins of Bawlmerese

A number of Bawlmer natives speak a form of American English sometimes referred to as Upper Chesapeake Adenoidal and commonly called Bawlmerese. Like any living language it is constantly evolving, but it shares its roots with working class accents found on the East Coast from Boston to Brooklyn to Philadelphia. All these forms of speech can be traced back to the Cockneys of London.

Working class people have often spoken a corrupted form of the language they share with the gentry. Limited educational opportunities and the pressures of earning a living often make acquiring "proper" speech a difficult task. In addition, a secret language offers certain advantages when you don't want the lords and ladies to know what you are saying about them.

"He ain got nao clays owen."

The speech patterns found in the Bawlmer of today are markedly different from those of even a few generations ago. This has been most significantly influenced by the northward migrations during the Great Depression and immediately after World War Two. The twang of the West Virginia hills and the drawl of the Deep South quickly blended into the stew of Bawlmerese.

The particular combination that has given Bawlmer its unique quality is a mixture of Cockney, German, and Italian, along with a variety of Southern American dialects and more than a touch of Central Europe.

2

 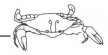

Hal baout dem O's?

It is appropriate that Bawlmer's favorite team is the Orioles, otherwise known as *de Oreos*, *de Oryuls*, or just *de O's*.

The "ao" pronunciation of long "o's" is perhaps the most classic example of Bawlmerese. Whether sung with force and vigor in the national anthem (*"AO, say does dat stor spangelt banner yet wabe?"*) or used in casual conversation (*"Ao ma Gawd, did chew see dat? He got de sem-ten split!"*) your pronunciation of "o" marks you as a native as surely as does your skill at disassembling crabs.

In pronouncing an American Standard long "o" the sound begins in the middle of the oral cavity. To achieve an accurate *"ao"* one must move the sound up and into the back of the mouth. Imagine a slightly offensive odor, wrinkle your nose, "squinch" your eyes slightly, and just say *"ao."*

There is a controversy among provincial linguists as to whether the Bawlmer *ao* has one or two syllables. In my mind this is like the argument over the difference in pronunciation of the words "bear" and "bare." I personally subscribe to the two-syllable school of thought, but hey, it's Bawlmer, Hon.

Hurry up and slow down

Certain regions are known for the speed of their speech. Visitors to New York often beg their hosts to slow down. New Yorkers visiting the South have been known to become hypertensive waiting for one syllable words to end. In Bawlmer, the south and the north meet in the mouths of its native speakers. Drawn out vowel sounds are an obvious example of southern influence. At the same time, consonants are often compressed and whole syllables seem to disappear in Bawlmerese.

For example, both the lazy multi-syllabic vowels of Georgia and the dulled and swallowed consonants of Brooklyn are found in the following characteristic sentence from a Middle River housewife:

"Ao ma Gawd, de maters er sao spensive in dis stooer."

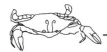 

Compare the same sentence in Standard American:

"Oh my God, the tomatoes are so expensive in this store."

The two syllables lost, one each in *tomatoes* and *expensive*, are replaced by three extra syllables in *Ao* (Oh), *sao* (so), and *stooer* (store). The sounds are simplified as in *de* (the) and *dis* (this) just as they might be in Brooklyn, but the delivery is much more relaxed.

Further examples of southern vowel influences can be heard in *dooer* (door), *flooer* (floor), and *mooer* (more).

Examples of northern influences on sound compression can be found in both internal and prepositional forms. The internal forms slur sounds in the middle of words as in *gummint* (government), *Blair* (Bel Air), *Beeno* (B & O), and *Murlin* (Maryland).

The prepositional forms drop initial vowels or consonants, almost like the dropped "aitches" of Cockney. Examples of dropped initial vowels would include *Naplis* (Annapolis), *speshly* (especially), and *mergency* (emergency). Instances of dropped initial consonants would include *tater* (potato), *mater* (tomato), and more recently *Intendo* (Nintendo).

This strange combination of speed and leisure is an extension of the Bawlmer lifestyle: "Make it simple and take it easy, Hon."

Where the L is it?

A sensitive issue when discussing Bawlmerese is the "Brokaw" effect. Many speakers of Bawlmerese have difficulty with their "l's." The sound is either dropped completely or transformed into a "w."

Unfortunately, this particular quality of speech is sometimes considered an impediment rather than merely a cultural manifestation. It should be considered no more of a disability than the Slavic pronunciation of "v" and "w." When one hears a particular sound in the home, the school, and the neighborhood, that sound becomes the standard or "proper" way to speak.

Examples of the elusive "l" would include *Coat* (Colt), *hep* (help), and *hoe* (hole). The transformed "l" is shown in *dowwer* (dollar), *cowwie* (collie), *trowwie* (trolley), and *tewwer* (teller).

Th - NOT!

Bawlmerese has little use for the "th" sound. It is generally replaced with "d", "f", or "v" sounds.

Like their cousins in New York, Bawlmer natives replace some initial "th's" with "d" as in *dese*, *dem*, and *dose*. The "f" for "th" is found at the beginning and end of words - *fin* (thin), *free* (three), *norf* (north), and *wurf* (worth). The middle "th" is replaced by a "v" sound as in *uvver* (other), *bovver* (bother), *favver* (father), and *norvern* (northern).

The builders of old Bawlmer must have been aware of this, as few of the older neighborhoods or landmarks have "th" in their names. Exceptions exist, such as *Linficum* and *Looferville*, but it took another generation of builders to give the Bawlmer area new, upscale place names to mispronounce.

New to the area, a number of recent home builders chose to add the word "garth" (an archaic term for a glen or meadow) to the name of an old upscale neighborhood. They hoped to cash in on an existing reputation and create instant familiarity, but names like "Somerset Garf (rhymes with barf)," somehow didn't quite capture the desired image.

 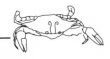
The de-provincialization of Bawlmer has brought us new names like *Woodard en Lofrup* and *De Paraplan* to join old familiars like *Woolwurf's* and *Misser Ray's Hair Weeb*. Some of the old names are gone now, like *Author's Bakry*, *de Sibic Senner*, and *de Noospos*, but the city lives on.

B for V

German immigrants made a significant impact on Bawlmer. Many Marylanders voted to make German the official language of the newly independent America.

Even though most of Bawlmer's German place names were erased during World War I (Redwood Street used to be German Street), church services are still performed in German at the Zion Lutheran Church next to City Hall and German family names are still prominent: Schaefer, Haussner, Hecht, Hochschild, Meyerhoff, Kraushaar, Mencken.

One of the most obvious influences of this heritage can be seen in the substitution of "b" for "v" throughout Bawlmerese. A few illustrations are *cubber* (cover), *ebry* (every), *Gobens* (Govans), and most germane - *ober* (over).

The language of medicine

Bawlmer has produced many famous names in medicine - Johns Hopkins, William Osler, William Halsted, Alfred Blalock, Helen Taussig, "Doc" Holliday ... the presence of several peculiarly Bawlmeristic medical terms should therefore come as no surprise.

"His larnix is jaggered."

For instance: *ammonia* (pneumonia), *anockalayshin* (inoculation), *aspern* (aspirin), *authoritis* (arthritis), *bronical* (bronchial), *carapracker* (chiropractor), *chicken pops* (chicken pox), *dennis* (dentist), *docker* (doctor), *eggs-ray* (X-ray), *genetic* (generic), *hosbiddle* (hospital), *infantigo* (impetigo), *larnix* (larynx), *pharnix* (pharynx), *pressperation* (perspiration), *prostrate* (prostate), *thamometer* (thermometer), *varse* (virus), and *vomick* (vomit).

X marks the spot

The "x" sound is special in Bawlmer. Like the "l" sound, it sometimes disappears, but it also replaces other sounds.

When it appears at the beginning of a word like except, explain, or expensive, it often transforms into an "s" sound as in *cept*, *splain*, or *spensive*.

In other situations, the "x" sound appears where it had not been before: *conjexture* (conjecture), *pixture* (picture), *inbetwixt* (in between), and *ax* (ask).

9

Native Renditions

To better illustrate both the pronunciation and the feeling of my native language, I have included several classic and original songs and poems transcribed into Bawlmerese. They should be sung or read aloud to fully appreciate their charm.

De Stor Spangelt Banner
by Francis Scott Key
(as sung at Orioles home games)

Ao say can yew see ba de don's early late,
What sao praddly we held at de twahlate's lass gleemin,
Hews broad strapes en brate stors, frew de pearlus fate,
Ore de ramparts we watched were sao gawwandly streamin?
En de roggets' red glare, de bums burstin in air,
Gabe proof frew de nate dat air flag was still dere.
AO say does dat stor spangelt ba-an-ner-er ye-ed way-abe,
Ore de la-ann ub de free en de haome ub de brabe.

PLAY BAW!

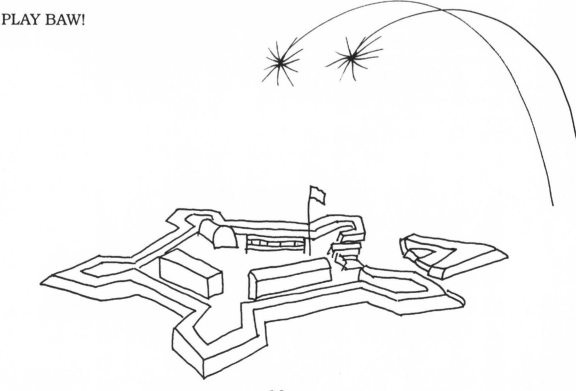

Bawlamer Coats Fate Song
Words and Music by
Jo Lombardi and Benjamin Klasmer
(as sung by Coats fans)

Less gao yew Bawlamer Coats,
En put dat baw acrost dat lon,
Sao, dribe owen yew Bawlamer Coats,
Gao in en strake lake latenin boats,
Fate! Fate! Fate!

Rear up yew Coats en less fate,
Crash frew en shao dem yer mate,
Fer Bawlamer en Muralin,
Yew will morch owen ta victory!

Casey at de Bat

by
Ernest L. Thayer
(as read by Buzzy Herkimer)

De aoutlook wudden brillyen fer de Mudville non dat day;
De scooer stud fooer ta two wif but one innin mooer ta play,
En when Cooney dod at firs, en Barrows did de same,
A pawl-lake sollence fell upowen de patrons ub de game.

A stragglin few got up ta gao in dip despurr. De ress
Clang ta dat haope which springs eternal in de yewman bress;
Dey fought, "If oney Casey could but get a whack at dat—-
We'd put up eeben money, wif Casey at de bat."

But Flynn preceded Casey, as did also Jimmy Blake,
En de former was a hewdew, en de latter was a cake;
So upowen dat stricken multeetood grim melancowwie sat;
For dere seemed but liddle chancet ub Casey gettin ta de bat.

But Flynn let drob a single, ta de wonderment ub awl,
En Blake, de much despahs`ed, tooer de cubber awf de baw;
En when de duss had liff`ed, en men sol what had occurred,
Dere was Jimmy safe at seconn en Flynn a-hugging fird.

Den ferm fibe talzon froats en mooer dere raose a lusty yell;
It rumbled frew de vowie, it rattled in de dell;
It pounded owen de mountain en ree-colled on de flat,
For Casey, matey Casey, was advancin ta de bat.

Dere was ease in Casey's manner as he stepped into his place;
Dere was prod in Casey's bearin en a smol lit Casey's face.
En when, respondin ta de cheers, he lately doffed his hat,
Nao stranger in de crowd could daout `twas Casey at de bat.

12

Ten falzon ahs were owen him as he rubbed his hants wif dirt;
Fibe talzon tongues applauded when he waped dem owen his shirt;
Den wowl de wrahvin pitcher grayon de baw into his hip,
Dee-fanse flashed in Casey's ah, a sneer curled Casey's lip.

En nal de lever-cubbered spear came hurtlin frew de air,
En Casey stood a-watchin it in haughty granjer dere.
Close bah de stordy batsman de baw unheeded sped—-
"Dat ain ma stoll," said Casey. "Strake one!" de umpar said.

Ferm de benches, black wif peepul, dere wen up a muffled rooer,
Lake de beatin ub de storm-wabes owen a stern en distan shooer;
"Kiw him! Kiw de umpar!" shaouted some one owen de stann;
En iss lakely dey'd have kilt him had not Casey raised his hann.

Wif a smol ub Christian charity great Casey's visage shaone;
He stilled de rosin chewmult; he bade de game gao owen;
He signaled ta de pitcher, en oncet mooer de dun spear flew:
But Casey still ignored it, en de umpar said "Strake two!"

"Fraud!" crod de maddened falzons, en echo answered "Fraud!"
But one scornful look ferm Casey en de audience was awed.
Dey saw his face graow stern en caold, dey saw his muskles strayon,
En dey knew dat Casey wudden led dat baw gao bah agayon.

De sneer has fled ferm Casey's lip, his teef er clinched in hate;
He payons wif crewel vollence, his bat upowen de pwate.
En nal de pitcher holes de ball, en nal he less it gao,
En nal de air is shattered wif de force ub Casey's blaow.

Ao, summair in dis faybered lann de sun is shannin brate;
De bann is playin summair, en summair horts er late,
En summair men er laughin, en liddle childern shaout;
But dere iss nao jooie in Mudville—-matey Casey has done strucked aout.

Take Me Aout ta de Baw Game
Lyrics by Jack Norworth
Music by Albert Von Tilzer

Take me aout ta de baw game
Take me aout wif de craowd
Buy me some peanuts en cracker jacks
Ah doan keer if Ah nebber get back

For iss rewt! rewt! rewt! for de haome team
If dey doan win iss a shame
En iss one! two! free strakes yer aout!
At de ol' baw game.

 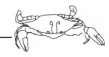

Owen fixin ta gao aout inna snao

Chimbleys er slick wif snao en ace
En de stoops er lookin speshly nace
When firs de flakes begin ta blao
In Bawlmer's Snao Mergency Race

It ain lake we neber seen snao
Jess when we do, we godda gao
Fer milk en bread, en lake dat dere
En Hon, doan ferget de Loddao

Sawlt trucks get sent aout ba de Mare
De wrecks is pallin up owen Blair
Ma bewts is sittin by de dooer
Ah knaow ma hat's rayon'cheer sumair

Ah'd lake ta stop en talk summooer
But nal iss tom ta stort de core
Iss molls ta gao afore de stooer
Yeah, molls ta gao afore de stooer

15

A Bisit ferm Sane Nicklus
by Clement C. Moore
(as read by Darfy Herkimer)

Twas de nate afore Crissmiss, en awl frew de haouse
Not a creature was stirrin, not eeben a maouse.
De stalkins was hung ba de chimbley wif care
In haopes dat Sane Nicklus soon 'ud be dere.

De childern was nestled awl snug in dere beds,
Wowl visions ub sugarplums danceted in dere heads.
En Mama in her kerchief en me in ma cap,
Had jess settled dayon fer a long winner's nap.

When aout owen de lawn dere araose sech a clabber
I spranged ferm ma bed ta see what was de matter.
Away ta de winder Ah flew lake a flash,
Tore open de shutters en frew up de sash.

De mewn owen de bress ub de new fawwen snao
Gabe de luster ub mid-day ta de objects blao,
When, what ta ma wondrin ahs shud appear,
But a minyacher sleigh, en eight tahnny reindeer,

Wif a liddle ol' drobber, sao lobbly en quick,
Ah knew in a moment it muss be Sane Nick.
Mooer rapid den iggles his corsers dey came,
En he whistled, en shaouted, en cawwed dem ba name.

"Nal, Dasher! nal, Danceter! nal, Pranceter en Vixen!
Owen Comet! owen Cewpid! owen, Donder en Blitzen!
Ta de top ub de porch! ta de top ub de waw!
Nal dash away! dash away! dash away awl!"

16

As drah leebs dat afore de wowld hurricen flah,
When dey meet wif an obstacle, mount ta de skah,
Sao up ta de haouse-top de corsers dey flew,
Wif de sleigh full ub teweys, en Sane Nicklus tew.

En den, in a twinklin, Ah heered owen de ruf
De prancetin en parrin ub each liddle huf.
As Ah drew in ma head, en was tornin arayon,
Dayon de chimbley Sane Nicklus came wif a bayon.

He was dressed awl in fur, ferm his head ta his foot,
En his clays was awl tornished wif ashes en sut;
A bunnel ub teweys he had flang owen his back,
En he looked lake a peddler jess op'nin his pack.

His ahs - hal dey twinkled! his dimples hal merry!
His cheeks was lake raoses, his naose lake a cherry!
His droll liddle mouff was drawed up lake a bao,
En de beard owen his chin was as what as de snao;

De stump ub a pop he held tate in his teef,
En de smaoke it encircled his head lake a reef;
He had a broad face en a liddle rayon bewwy,
Dat shook, when he laughed, lake a bowfool ub jewwy.

He was chubby en plump, a rate jowwy ol' elf,
En Ah laughed when Ah saw him, in spot ub maseff;
A wink ub his ah en a twiss ub his head,
Soon gabe me ta nao Ah had nuffn ta dread;

He spoke not a word, but went straight ta his work,
En filled awl de stalkins; den torned wif a jerk,
En layin his finger upsod ub his naose,
En gibbin a nod, up de chimbley he raose;

He sprang ta his sleigh, ta his team gabe a whistle,
En away dey awl flew lake de dayon ub a thistle.
But Ah heerd him exclaim, ere he drobe aout ub sate,
"Happy Crissmiss ta awl en ta awl a good nate."

17

CRISSMISS CAROLS
(as sung by the PenLucy Singers)

Sollent Nate

Sollent Nate, Haoly Nate
Awl is calm, awl is brate.
Rayon yon Birgin, Muvver en chowld,
Haoly Infink, sao tender en molld,
Sleep in hebenly peace,
Sleep in hebenly peace.

Ao Liddle Tayon ub Beflum

Ao, liddle tayon ub Beflum
Hal still we see dee la!
Abub dye deep en dreamless sleep
De sollent stors gao ba;
Yet in dye dork streets shineff
Dye eberlassin Late;
De haopes en fears ub awl de years
Are met in dee ta-nate.

Gawd Ress Yew Merry Gennelmen

Gawd ress yew merry gennelmen,
Let nuffn yew dismay,
Fer Jesus Chriss, air Sabeyer,
Was borned on Crissmiss day,
Ta sabe us awl ferm Satan's pare
When we was gonned astray.
Ao, toddins ub compert en jooie, compert en jooie!
Ao, toddins ub compert en jooie!

BAWLMERESE-ENGLISH DICTIONARY

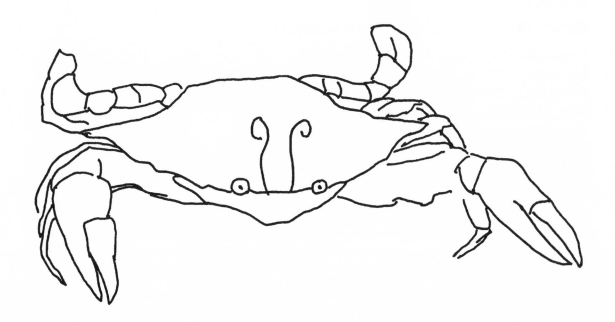

A

abenoo	avenue. "Ah'm goan up owen Eassern *abenoo*. OK, Hon?"
accordeen	accordion. "Ma bruvver lake ta dod when he got his firs *accordeen*, but nal he's playin "Lady ub Spain" at ma weddin."
ace	ice. "Ah lake ta broke ma ess when Ah slipped owen dat *ace*."
acebox	see *fergerator, fergidair*.
acrost	across. "Darfy can't gao *acrost* de Hannober Street bridge wifaout shettin her ahs."
admarred	admired. "Suzee oweez *admarred* Joan Jett's clays."
affernoon	afternoon. "Ma Sunny *affernoons* ain been de same since de Coats leff."
affleet, affaleet	athlete.
afore	before.
af(r)ican	afghan. "Ah got a lubbly *african* ferm de rubbage sale ober ta de Loofran Church."
agayon	oncet mooer.
Ah	I. "*Ah* wish yew wooden do dat."
ah	eye. see *squinch*.
Ah'd	I'd. see *Odd*.
Ah'm	I'm. "*Ah'm* fixin ta gao downy O's game."
aholt	hold tightly. "Hey Hon, grab *aholt* ub dis fer me."

ahreddy	already. "Dat sem pin shudda falled ober *ahreddy*."
Ahreen	Irene.
ain	ain't. "*Ain* de beer caold!"
air	there. "*Air* yew gao!"
air	our. "We spent awl *air* money owen O's tickets"
Airao	Arrow. Bawlmer beer of the past.
airs	hours. singular: *nair*.
airy	every. see *ebry*.
airyul	aerial. see *TB*.
Allanic	see *Ayshin, downy*.
alob	not dead.
amblanz	ambulance.

"Yew better get de amblanz, de baby's comin rate nal!"

amember	remember. "D'yew *amember* Read's? Harley's? FooFair? Author's Bakry?"
ammal	animal. see *draff, elfin, line, tagger, zeeber,* and *zew*.
ammonia	pneumonia. "De docker says Ah got bronical *ammonia*. Got a late?"

Annarunnel	Anne Arundel (County). also see *Naplis*.
anfem	anthem. "Ao say can yew see..." see *nashnul*.
Anf'ny	Anthony.
annis	honest. "*Annis* Awfser, Ah oney had one beer."
anockalayshin	shot in the arm.
annuver	another. "D'yew fink wull ged *anuvver* football team?"
Aoberlee	Overlea. see also *Oberlee*.
aok	oak. see *pawsun*.
Ao's	O's. "Hal baout dem *Ao's*?"
aokay	okay.
aout	out. "Be keerful Hon, iss hort ta get beer stains *aout* ub dis polstry."
Aozmobill	Oldsmobile.
aparmen	department. Far *Aparmen*, Pleece *Aparmen*, Helf *Aparmen*.
A-rabber	produce salesman with horse-drawn cart.
architexture	two-story brick rowhouses with marble front steps.
arful	bad but not *turble*.
Arlin	Ireland. see *Arsh*.
Armadeus	Mozart's middle name.
arn	aren't. "*Arn* chew gunna eat dat?"
arn	iron. "Hey Hon, when er yew gunna *arn* ma shirt?"
arnjoos	brekfess drink.
Arsh	Irish. "Ebrybody's *Arsh* owen Sane Paddy's Day."

23

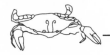 

arthur	author. "Dere's lossa *arthurs* ferm Bawlmer: Leon Uris, Russell Baker, Ort Donnaben…"
asfelt	asphalt. "Dey cubbert up awl de ol' trowwie tracks wif *asfelt*."
asperagrass	asparagus. "If yew eat *asperagrass*, yer pee smells funny."
aspern	aspirin. "Ah yewjally need free er fooer *asperns* affer Ah come back ferm de bowwin owie."
assessories	accessories. "De Pep Buoys sells oughtao *assessories*."
ast	ask. "Are yew gunna *ast* Edif ta de dance?"
attackted	attacked.

"Buzzy got *attackted* by yeller jackets!"

Austin	Ostend (Street).
Author	*Author* Donnaben, *Author* Godfrey, King *Author*…
authoritis	arthritis. "Yew should orter put dis sab owen yer *authoritis*."

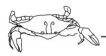 

awf	off. "Get *awf* dat stoop!"
awfser	officer. "Annis *Awfser*, Ah doan nao hal dat got dere."
awfus	office. where you play the football pool.
awl	all. "*Awl* Ah want fer Crissmiss is ma two fernt teef."
awl	oil. "Ma favver's Caddylak took sis cortsa *awl*!"
ax	ask. "De uvver guy ahreddy *axed* me baout dat."
axdint	not owen porpuss.
ayf	eighth. **8th**
ayshin	ocean. see *downy, Allanic*.
ayugs	eggs. see *Easser, harballed*.
azaleum	azalea. see *Flare Mort*.

B

Babe Roof	dam Yankee.
baffrum	bathroom. "Dis hase needs mooer den one *baffrum*."
ball	to raise the temperature of a liquid until it becomes a gas.
bansol	bandsaw. "If yew doan watch aout yell cutcher finger awf wif dat *bansol*."
Bao	Boh(emian). Native beer, also *nashnul*.

baout   about. "Me en yer muvver been married *baout*... hal old er yew nal?"

bard   borrowed. "Sumpn old, sumpn new, sumpn *bard*, sumpn blew."

Bawlmer   common form. Home of the Orioles, Queen City of the Patapsco Drainage Basin, home of hand painted window screens, steamed crabs, and marble steps, duckpin capital of the world, Charm City, and the home at one time or another of Spiro T. Agnew, Philip Berrigan, John Wilkes Booth, Buddy Dean, Kelson "Chop-Chop" Fisher, Dashiell Hammett, Alger Hiss, Billie Holiday, "Doc" Holliday, Joan Jett, Jeffrey Levitt, Loudy Loudenslager, Thurgood Marshall, Teddy McKeldin, H. L. Mencken, Madeline Murray, Ogden Nash, Wally Orlinsky, Edgar Allan Poe, Hyman Pressman, William Donald Schaefer, Abe Sherman, Wallis Warfield Simpson, Blaze Starr, John Waters, and Frank Zappa.

Bawlamer   semi-formal.

Bawltymooer   formal.

Bebberly   Beverly.

Beeno   B & O. archaic, generic for railroad.

beero   bureau. "Ah fink Ah leff ma bowwin shews unnerneef de *beero*."

Beflum   Bethlehem. ...Steel, see *dePoint*.

Belbadeer   Belvedere (Avenue).

Bel'way   Beltway.

bestess   better than best.

bewt   boot.

binness   business. "Yew ain got nao *binness* messin wif ma fings."

 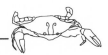

birfday	birthday. "We got awl tanked up en went ta deBlock owen ma eighteemf *birfday*."
Blair	Bel Air. road or town.
blao	blow. "If yew put too much air in dem tars dell *blao* up!"
blao	below. "De win chill muss be twenny *blao*."
bleebit	believe it. "Ah doan *bleebit*!"
bleef	belief. "In Bawlmer we doan attack nobody's *bleefs*, eeben if dere wrong."
blew crabs	buckrams, busters, culls, doublers, jimmies, megalops, paper shells, peelers, soft shells (hotels, primes, jumbos, slabs, whales), and sooks.
bloon	balloon.
B'n'G	BG&E. Bawlmer Gas'n'Lectric

bobwar	barbed wire. see *far*.
booerd	board. "Jimmy got wacked inna head wif a *booerd* when he was a kit, en he ain bin de same eber since."

booshela	a bushel of...crabs, corn, tamaters...
borned	born. "Ah was *borned* in Waberly, hal baout chew Hon?"
borry	borrow. "Ah'm tard ub yew *borryin'* ma core keys."
bovver	bother. "Doan it *bovver* yew when iss so yewmid yer glasses fog up?"
bowwin	bowling. see *ducks, owie.*
boy	buoy. "Foller de *boys* en yew woan get loss."
brate	bright. "He mate be big, but he ain too *brate.*"
breath	breadth. see *lenth.*
brekfess	meal before brunch.
bronical	bronchial. see *ammonia.*
bruvver	brother. "Billy is mooer den jess Cal's *bruvver.*"
bub	see *late.*
bum	bomb. "...en de roggets red glare, de *bums* borstin in air..."
bummerstigger	bumpersticker. "Pro-Chowld, Pro-Fambly, Pro-Bowwer"
buoy	boy. "Jess a cupla de *buoys* er comin ober."
burguler	burglar. "*Burgulers* beware! Ah'm mental!!"
Byewk	Buick.
byewdy	beauty. see *skewl.*
byskool	bicycle.

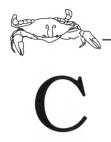 

C

Cafflick	Catholic. see *prokyul*.
cal	cow. (Mebbe dass hal come he's oweez sellin' milk.)
Calbert	Calvert. Founding fambly ub Murlin. see *cownny*.
calor, cuwwer	color. Bawlmer's colors are black and orange, just like the Orioles.
Calorado	Colorado.
calvary	soldiers on horses to the rescue.
cammer	camera. see *fillum*.
cantylope	cantaloupe.
caold	cold. see *ain*.
cemetree	cemetery.
cept	except. "...ebryfing *cept* de kitchen zink."
Cherman	German.
chew	you. "Oltnao bout *chew*, Hon..."
chewmult	tumult. "He stilled de rosin *chewmult*, he bade de game gao owen..." *Casey at de Bat*.
Chewzdee	Tuesday.
chicken pops	chicken pox.
chimbley	chimney. see *Sandy Clouse*.
Cholly	Charlie. Eckman, Byrd, Lau, de Tuner.
chowld	child. see *kidneygorden*.

29

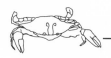
clabber	clatter. "When aout owen de lawn dere araose sech a *clabber*…" — *A Bisit ferm Sane Nicklus*.
clays	clothes. "Eeben when Blaze Storr took awf her *clays* she was still a classy lady."
cloff	cloth. "Tarzan oney wore a lawn *cloff*."
Clumya	Columbia. see *Harrid* cownny.
Coats	Colts. "Less gao yew Bawlamer *Coats*, da da da da da da da da-a-ah."

BAWLMER COATS

Sept. 7, 1947 - Mar. 28, 1984

complected	complexioned. "Suzee can't take too much sun, she's too late *complected*."

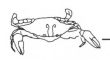
commewny	community. "She's a graddyate ferm Teddy McKeldin *Commewny* Cowwitch."
conjexture	conjecture. "Annis, Awfser, Ah been *conjexturin* baout dat maseff."
core	car. as in *Monny Corelao*.
corm beef	corned beef. see *sammidge*.
cornish	cornice. Bawlmer architextural terminology.
cort	quart. "Coat Fordy Fibe tase de bess ferm a *cort* bottle."
corter	quarter. "Venchully, awl *corters* end up in video games."

Corters

c

council	cancel. "Soon's de firs snao flake hits de grayon, ebryfing gets *counciled*."

cownny	county. Bawlmer, Harrid, Annarunnel, Harfert, Calbert...
cowwieflare	cauliflower.
cowwitch	college. Calbert Haw, Dundock, Notra Dom, Siddy.
crimull	criminal. people what do *croms*.
crissanfeum	chrysthanthemums. see *Flare Mort*.
Crissmiss	Christmas. see *Sandy Clouse*.
crom	crime. what *crimulls* do.
cron	crying. "Hal come dat liddle chowld's *cron*?"
crupt	corrupt. see *gummint*.
cubber	cover. "Soon's Ah win de Loddao, Ah'm gettin me some new wheel *cubbers*."
cubbert	covered. "Whadda yew mean Ah'm not *cubbert*? It was oney a liddle far."
cubbert	cupboard. "We got de new *cubberts* ober at Monkey Wars."
culcher	culture. see *TB*.
cupla	couple of. "Ah oney had a *cupla* beers."
cut awf	turn off. de lates, de gas, de wooder. see *wennup*.
cway	clay. see *sawl*.
cwub session	club section. see *mucky-muck*.

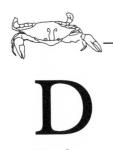 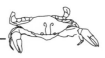

D

Darfy	Dorothy.
Darse	Doris.
dass	that's. "*Dass* ma foot yer steppin owen, Hon."
dao	though. "Ah lake bagels eeben *dao* dey come ferm New York."
dat	that. look at *dis*.
dawfin	dolphin. see *quairyum*. "Oops! dere sick agayon."
dayon	down. "Hey Hon, put dat *dayon* owen de grayon"
de	the.
dell	they'll, there'll. "*Dell* tell yew differnt but *dell* neber be anuvver Jawnny U."
dePoint	see *Sparris* Point, *Beflum* Steel, company town.
dem	them. "Ah got *dem* at Wullwurf's."
dennis	dentist. Doc Holliday —- Bawlmer's most famous *dennis*.
dere	there, they're. "*Dere* yew gao. *Dere* rippin up de payment agayon."
dese	these. look at *dose*.
dest	desk. "Moob dat *dest* ober here, Hon."
Dezember	December.
din	didn't. "Buzzy *din* tell me yew was so byewdyfull."

dis	this. look at *dat*.
Dizzy Whirl	Disney World.
doan	don't. see *nebber*.
docker	doctor.
dod	died. see *Pao, Babe Roof, Jawn Hokkins*.
dog pond	has nothing to do with swimming canines.
doll	dial. see *phane*.
Donal	Donald. Schaefer, Trump, Duck.
dooer	door. "Here, Ah'll hold dat *dooer* fer yew, Hon."
dooerstoop	doorstep. see *morble*.
dork	dark. "It was a *dork* en stormy nate."
dose	those. look at *dese*.
downy	down to the. see *Ayshin*

DOWNY AYSHIN

34

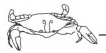 

dowwer	dollar. "De tickets er a corter each, free fer a *dowwer*."
draff	de tawwess ammal in de zew.
drar, drawl	draw.
draring, drawling	drawing.
Drewd Hill	Druid Hill.
Drewdl Park	Druid Hill Park.
drobber	driver. "Wir'd yew get yer *drobber's* license, in a box ub Cracker Jacks?"
Drooslem	Jerusalem.
drownded	very drowned.
druckstooer	drugstore. "Hey Hon, wowl yer at de *druckstooer*, get me a can ub Ol' Bay."
dubya	W.
duck	duct. as in *duck* tape.
ducks	duckpins. see *bowwin, owie*.
duddney?	doesn't he? "He looks jess lake Elvis, *duddney*?"
Dundock	Dundalk.
dune	doing. "Whatcha *dune*, Hon?"
Dwanie Vowie	go ahead and say it.
d'yew	do you? "*D'yew* bleeb dat Orty Donnaben? He's sumpn, inny?"

E

Easser	Easter. As in "Mary Sue *Easser* Ayugs."
Eassern, eastrin	eastern. *Hah Skewl, Shooer, Abenoo.*
ebber	ever. "Doan *ebber* rub yer ahs rate affer eatin crabs."
ebry	every. "*Ebry* baby borned in Bawlmer naos hal ta pick crabs."
ebryfing	everything. "Ma bruvver went ta truck drobber skewl en *ebryfing*."
eeben	even. "*Eeben* de crabs crod when de Coats leff."
eebnen	evening.

"...sittin owen de stoop ub an eebnen."

eever	either. "*Eever* s—t er get awf de pot."
ek setra	et cetera. "...en sao owen en sao forf."
elfin	de biggess ammal in de zew.
en	and.
er	or, are. "*Er* dey airs, *er er* dey yers?"
erf	earth. "De plant we lib owen."
ersters	see *urshters*.
ess	ass. see *ace*.
excape	escape. see *far*.
exihilarated	accelerated. "When de truck hit de ace it *exhilirated* lake a hase afar."
exlint	excellent. "De urshters er *exlint* dis year."
exter	extra. "Gimme some *exter* graybee owen dose frahs, Hon."

 F

falzon	thousand. see *talzon, ten hunnert*.
fambly	family. Dere's naoplace lake haome.
Fanksgibben	Thanksgiving. see *hollyday*.
far	fire. "Dey storted dat tar *far* too fore ferm de bobwar."

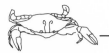 

Farbird	Firebird.
fard	fired. see *hard*.
fard	forehead. Inbetwixt yer ahs en yer hair.
farlarm	fire alarm.
farmin	fireman.
farner	foreigner.
farn gin	fire engine.
farst	forest. see *far*.
favver	father. "Ma *favver* learned me awl baout bowwin."
faw	fall. see *leebs, sprang*.
Febrerry	February. see *snao, mergency*.
fer	for. "We been lookin *fer* yew."
fergerator, fergidair	refrigerator. see *acebox*.
ferm	from. "Ah'm *ferm* Pigtayon."
fernt	front. see *stoop*.
few pump	fuel pump. see *core, wennup*.

fibe five.
fiff fifth.
fitteem fifteen.
fitty fifty.

fill	feel. "Buzzy doan *fill* too good. He missed de Loddao ba one number."
fillum	film. "Yew can't take nao pixtures wifaout nao *fillum*."
fin	thin. "Ma, ma, ma, din yew get *fin*?"
fing	thing. "Gimme dat *fing*!"

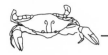

fink	think. "Yer in Bawlmer nal Hon, doan *fink* baout it."
firs	first.
firsty	thirsty. "Ah get matey *firsty* ba de forf innin."
Firzdee	Thursday.
fixin	planning. "Hey Hon, we're *fixin* ta gao crabbin. Hal baout chew?"
flayber	flavor. see *jore, summooer.*
flah	fly. also zipper.
Flarda	Florida.
flare	flower. Black Odd Suzee's.
Flare Mort	Flower Mart. rite of spring.

flitter	fritter. see *urshter.*
flooer	floor. see *grayon.*

foal	foil. as in luminum *foal*.
fonlall	father-in-law. see *munlall*.
foller	follow. "Annis Awfser, he *follered* me in here."
fond	find. "He cudden *fond* it naowar."
fonnly	finally. "Wayne *fonnly* passed de GED."
fooer **fordy** **forf**	four. forty. fourth. **4**
fool	full. "Nao mooer fer me, Hon. Ah'm *fool*. Well, mebbe jess a liddle peesa dat lemoran pah."
ford	forward.
fore	far. see *far*.
Forster	Foster (Street).
frao	throw. "Dat Osun sher can *frao* de baw."
fraon	thrown, throne. Past tense of *frao*. also see *tawlet*.
free **fird** **firteem** **firty**	three. third. thirteen. thirty. **3**
fret	threat. "Dass a promise, not a *fret*."
froat	throat. "Rar urshters slod rate dayon yer *froat*."
Froddy	Friday. "De day de iggle flahs."
futha	farther, further. "Doan gao nao *futha*."

G

ga hed	go ahead. "Yew jess *ga hed* Hon. Ah'll be aokay."
gao	go. see *Coats*.
Gawd	as in "Ao ma ..."
genetic	generic. "Gimme summa dat *genetic* penicillin, Doc."
gess	gets. "Firs one in *gess* de winder seat."
giff	gift.

"Oltnao, Hon, Ah oweez fought beer made de perfick giff."

Gobens	Govans.
goff	golf.
goldie	goalie.
gorden	garden. see *maters, skorsh, cantylopes, cowwieflare*.
grabble	gravel.

41

granite	granted. "Doan take nuffn fer *granite*, Hon."
grayon	ground. see *flooer*.
Greenmont	Greenmount (Abenoo).
grosher	grocer.
groshries	groceries. Chips, sammidges, pickles, tater salad, en tawlet paper.
Gubner	Governor. see *Naplis*.
gull	girl. no age limit.
gummint	government. as in "goddam..."
gun	gone. see *Coats*.
Gunfer	Gunther. Another Bawlmer beer of the past.
gunna	going to. "Didja hear? Shirl's buoy, liddle Waller's *gunna* gao ta de Nabel Cademy."
gymanasium	where de affaleets practice gymanastics.

H

Habberdy Grace **Habberdy Grah** **Habberdy Grass** **Hahvah de Grace** **Hahvah de Grah** **Hahvah de Grass** **Hava de Grace** **Hava de Grah** **Hava de Grass**	Havre de Grace

haddy!	howdy!
hah	high. see *ruf, skewl, tare, taw, tet*.
hal	how. "*Hal* was Ah spoza nao?"
hal come	why. "*Hal come* dey make fun ub de way Ah talk?"
hao	hoe. see *gorden*.
haome	home. see *Bawlmer*.
haouse, hase	house. see *rao*.
harballed	hard boiled. Eever ayugs er Mickey Spillane.
harble	lake *turble* but worse.
hard	hired. see *fard*.
Harfert	Harford (Road). see *cownny*.
Harrid	Howard (Street). see *cownny*.
hays	hose.
hebby	heavy. "Gimme a booshela' *hebby* crabs, Hon."
heliocopter	whirly bird.
helf	health. see *aparmen, hosbiddle*.
hep	help. "Lemme *hep* yew wif dat, Hon."
hoe	hole. "It wen rate frew de *hoe*."
ho, ho, ho, ho, ho!	stop!
holasec	see *wayasec, waymint*.
Hollintayon	Highlandtown.
Hollyday	see *Crissmiss, Fanksgibben*.

Hon   Honey, dear, buddy, pal, and more

hordware	see *stooer*.
hosbiddle	hospital. Jawn Hokkins, Bon Secure, Siddy, Union Moryul, Souff Bawlmer, Sane Agess, Sane Jao, Norf Charles, GMBC.

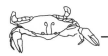 
100

hunnert	hundred.
hut	hot. see *tempcher, yewmid, wevver*.
hygeraniums	hydrangea. see *Flare Mort*.

I

ideer	idea. "Yew got any mooer smort *ideers*, Hon?"
Igger	Eager (Street).
iggle	eagle. see *Froddy*.
ignernt	ignorant. "Some people er sao *ignernt*."
ijut	idiot. see *maroon, yahoo*.
inbetwixt	(in) between. "Clumbya's *inbetwixt* Warshnin en Bawlmer."
infantigo	impetigo. chowld's skin disease.
injin	engine. see *mowder*.
Inlish	English. De langwich spoke ba Bawlamorons, sorta.
innertayment	entertainment. see *O's, TB*.
innit?	don't you agree? "It sher is yewmid, *innit*?"
inny?	isn't he? "Dat Boog Pal's rilly sumpn, *inny*?"
insparred	inspired. "Dat was some *insparred* bowwin, Waller."

45

Intendo   Nintendo. Zelda Free, Sooper Mario Worl ...

iss	it's. "*Iss* a wonder yew stayed alob dis long."
iss'n'at	this and that. en sao forf, en sao owen, ek setra.
ivory	ivy. "Watch aout fer de pawsun *ivory*."

J

jaggered	jagged. "De payment in yer sodwalk is *jaggered*."
Janes	Jones. *Janes* Faws.

Janyerry January. see *snao, mergency*.

jawn join. "Hal can Ah *jawn* de morchin ban?"

Jawn John. Unitas. see *Coats*.

Jawn Hokkins Johns Hopkins.

jeet? did you eat? "*Jeet*, Hon?"

jess just. "*Jess* a minute, Hon."

jew? did you? "*Jew* put up yer screems yet, Hon?"

jewry jewelry.

jografee geography.

Jopper Joppa. road or tayon.

jore jar. "Sher, Ah'll trah a *jore* ub dat crab flaybered peanut butter."

K

Kaffy	Kathy
keerful	careful.
kemcool	chemical. "Ah lub Tacey Cakes eeben if dere fool ub *kemcools*."
kidneygorden	kindergarten. see *chowld, kits*.
kilt	killed. past tense of *kiw*.
kits	kids. see *muvver*.
kiw	kill. As Milton Berle said, "I'll *kiw* you a miwwion times."
Kreer	Korea, career. see *kroddy*.
kroddy	karate. see *Kreer*.

L

lake	like.
larnix	larynx. see *pharnix*.
Laska	Alaska.
late	light. see *hebby, bub*.
laundried	laundered. "If yew ladies ain too busy can Ah get ma shirts *laundried*?"

48

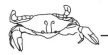 

lawn	loin. see *cloff*.
learn	teach. "Dat'll *learn* yew."
lectric	electric. see *late, wennup*.
leeb	leave, let, allow. "Want chew *leeb* it be, Hon?"
leebs	leaves. see *faw*.
leginamint	legitimate. see *gummint?*
lem	eleven. see *sem*.
lemoran	lemon meringue. *pah*.
lenth	length. "He slud de *lenth* ub de bar."
let owen	show. "Doan *let owen* dat yew seed me, Hon."
levver	leather. "Chew see ma *levver* bowwin bag, Hon?"
liberry	library. de Pratt.
liddle	little. see *lig, Itly, mooer*.
LiddleItly	Little Italy.
lig	league. see *Murcan, liddle*.
liggle	legal. "If Steeben Elmolls says iss *liggle* it muss be."
line	de ammal in de zew wif de biggess rooer.
Linficum	Linthicum.
lissen at	pay attention to. "Dese kits doan *lissen at* naoboby naomooer."
lobble	liable. see *liggle*.
lobbly	lively.

Loch Raben	Loch Raven (Avenue). also see *rezavore*.
Loddao	Lotto.

lom	lime. see *sawl*.
Looferville	Lutherville.
loose	lose. see *Coats*.
loss	lost. see *Warshnin*.
lub	love. see *O's*.
Lumberd	Lombard (Street).

M

ma	my. "*Ma, ma, ma,* ain yew sumpn?"
macadmium	macadam. see *asfelt*.
macely	mostly. "*Macely*, we gao crabbin ober ta Mill Ribber, Hon."
maffmatics	see *rifmetic*.
Maircan	American. One more Bawlmer beer of the past. also see *Noose*.
manooer	manure. see *tamater*.
Marhoff	Meyerhoff. see *sympathy*.
maroon	Dumber than a moron. see *ijut, yahoo*.
mary	Mary, marry, merry.
mater	tomato. see *tamater*.
maxium	maximum.
maw	mall. Wot Morsh, Skyurtee, Owens Mill, Yewdawood, de Garry...
meddle	metal. "Hey Hon, did Ah eber show yew de *meddle* plate in ma head?"
meeyun	million. as gibben away ba Mockle Anf'ny owen "De *Meeyunaire*."

Melhawk   Mohawk.

*"If dis Melhawk
doan tick awf ma ol' man
Ah doan nao what will."*

Mercree	Mercury.
mere	mirror. *"Mere, mere,* owen de waw..."
mergency	emergency. see *snao.*
mezaleen	mezzanine. "Yewtsa be yew could get a seat in de *mezaleen,* but nal iss fool ub mucky-mucks."
mill	middle. "Jess frao de baw downa *mill* ub de owie, Hon."
minium	minimum.
minrul	mineral. "Is it ammal, veggible, er *minrul*?"
Mockle	Michael.
moll	mile. "Warshnin is baout fordy *molls* ferm Bawlmer."
mollage	mileage. "Ma *mollage* wen up affer Ah fonnly fount de oberdrob."
mon	mine. "Hey! Dose crabs er *mon*!"
monament	monument. see *Warshnin.*
Monkey Wars	Montgomery Wards.
Monny Corelao	Monte Carlo.
moob	move. "Doan *moob*! Dere's a yeller jacket owen yer ...Goddim! ...Sorry baout dat."

moobies	movies. see *thee-ater, maw.*
mooer	more. "Wadda yew mean dere ain nao *mooer* crabs?"
morble	marble. see stoop.
Morch	March. Spring training.
morket	market. *Blair, Lessinin.*
moryul	memorial. see *stadyum, O's, Coats.*
mowdersickle	motorcycle.
M.R.	them are. (Ayshin Siddy chapter).
mucky-muck	one of the privileged few. see *cwub session.*
munf	month.
munlall	mother-in-law. see *fonlall.*
Murca	America.
muriel	mural. as in Heironimus.
Murlin	Maryland. "De haome ub plezzen libbin."
muvver	mother. see *sane.*

N

nace	nice. "Hey! Be *nace* ta yer bruvver!"
nair	an hour. plural: *airs.*
nal	now. "*Nal, nal,* he's oney trahin ta hep."
nao	no. see *Coats.*
naowir	nowhere. "Ain *naowir* lake Bawlmer."

Naplis	Annapolis. see *gummint, gubner*.
nashnul	national. as in *Bao, anfem*.
nate	night. "De Late Rail gets rilly crowded affer a *nate* game, Hon."
Natty Bao	National Bohemian.
naybee	navy. see *Naplis*.
nebber	never. "Sheree, dis calor's *nebber* gunna come aout!"
nex	next. "*Nex* tom, Ah'll hold de keg en yew hold de pitcher."
non	nine.
nondy	ninety.
nonf	ninth.
Noose Maircan	News American.
Noose Pos	News Post. gone but not forgotten.
noosepaper	newspaper. "De Sun."
norf	north. Talzon, Dwanie Vowie, Looferville.
Norvern	Northern. Hah skewl, bagels, maple surp, snao.
notarerry	notary. A seccerterry who can notarize?
nuffn	nothing. "Doan worry baout it, it ain *nuffn*."
nuculer	nuclear.

9

"Ah been workin dayon ta de nuculer plant fer free years nal. Hal come yew ast?"

 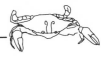

O (AO)

ober	over. see *Cherman*.
Oberlee	Overlea. see *Aoberlee*.
Odd	I'd. "*Odd* lake free dozen crabs en a Loddao, Hon."
Oddlewowld	Idlewild.
Okkentrowwie	Auchenteroly. Test for radio and TV reporters new to Bawlmer, "Ouch-en-te-rolly?"
oll	aisle.
ollin	island.
oltnao	I don't know. "*Oltnao* bout chew Hon, but Ah fill lucky. Gimme nuvver Loddao."
oncet	once. "Ah been ta Warshnin *oncet*. Got loss."
oney	only. "If *oney* dey'd leff us de name…"
ordiance	ordinance. "Scuse me Hon, but yer in vollation ub free differnt *ordiances*."
Oregon Drob	Argonne Drive.
ormy	army. "Gao Naybee, beat *Ormy*."
orning	awning.
ort	art. "Murlin *Ort* Insitute."
orter	ought to. "Yew *orter* take dat Injanaplis shirt awf."

Oryuls   Orioles. Brooks, Frank, Boog, Earl, Cal, Eddie, Jim, Gus, Milt, Hoyt, Paul, Rick, Luis, Willie, Curt, Tippy, Elrod, Andy, Chuck Thompson...

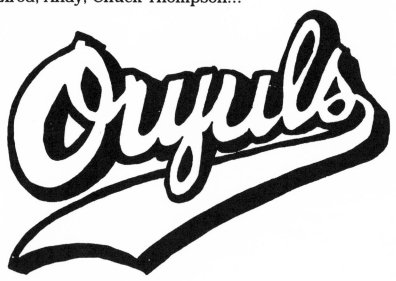

Oreos	More Orioles.
O's	Never too many Orioles.
oughtamobill	automobile. see *core*.
oughtao	auto. Wessern Oughtao.
Ow	Al.
Ow-bert	Albert.
Ow-ferd	Alfred.
Ow-ma	Alma.
owen	on. "He jess wen *owen*, en *owen*, en *owen*..."
oweez	always. "Jimmy's *oweez* got a caold sispack."

owie	alley. see *bowwin, ducks*.
oyz	always. "War yew *oyz* gibbin me a hort tom?"

P

padder	powder. see *baffrum*.
pah	pie. see *lemoran*.
pall	pile. see *leebs, faw*.
paller	parlor. "Yew ladies yews de *paller*. Wull gao downa rumpus rum."
pallet, pollet	pilot.
pancake	pound cake.
Pao, Eggar Awwen	Poe, Edgar Allan. ...dod inna Bawlmer gutter.
paramour	power mower. see *Monkey Wars*.
Paraplan	Power Plant. see *poplar* ...NOT!
parasol	power saw. see *hosbiddle*.
Parkites	Park Heights.
partial post	parcel post.
Parts	Pirates.
Patapsico	Patapsco.
patater	potato. see *tater*.
pawsun	poison. see *aok, ivory*.
payment	pavement. see *sodwalk, macadmium, asfelt*.
pearl	peril. "De loff ub a Poh-leece is filled wif *pearls*."

peemoss	peat moss.
peepot	peat pot.
perfick	perfect. "Dat's jess *perfick*. Nal yew look jess lake Princess Dah."
pershoot	parachute. What yew haope de pallet doan need.
pertickler	particular. "Doan be too *pertickler* Hon, er dere woan be none leff."
petition	partition. "If yew two buoys doan quat dayon, Ah'll put a *petition* rate dayon de mill ub yer rum."
phane	phone.
piller	pillow.
Pissburg	Pittsburgh. see *Parts*.
pitcher, pixture	picture.
Plaski	Pulaski (Highway).
plate	polite. "He shooer was *plate*, fer a New Yorker."
pleece	police. mooer den one.

PLEECE

Plimiff	Plymouth.
plooshin	pollution. see *Sparris* Point, *sut*.
pockeybook	purse.
poh-leece	police. one.

POH-LEECE

polstry	upholstery.
pop	pipe.
poplar	popular. O's.
popular	poplar. trees.
porple	purple.
prah	pry. "Ah din mean ta *prah* Hon, jess curious."
prallum	problem. "Yew got a *prallum* wif dat?"
praps	perhaps. see *prolly*.
prarty	priority. "Firs crabs en beer, den cable TB - nao, firs cable TB, den crabs en beer - nao..."

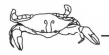
precint	precinct. see *Pleece*.
prentzel	pretzel.
president	present. "We got dis *president* speshul fer yew, Hon."
pressperation	perspiration. see *yewmid*.
prod	pried. "He *prod* it awf wif a screwdrobber."
prokyul	parochial. see *Cafflick*.
prolly	probably. "Wull *prolly* get anuvver team, doancha fink?"
pronounciation	pronunciation. "Er yew sher dass de rate *pronounciation*?"
prostrate	prostate. see *hosbiddle*.
pruin	prune.
purdy	see *byewdy*.
Purdybuoy	Prettyboy. see *rezavore*.
pyana	piano.

q-ponz	coupons.
quairyum	aquarium. nashnul ub cooerse.

quat	quiet. "Iss too *quat* in Waberly dese days."

QUAT NAL

R

race beef	roast beef. see *sammidge*.
Rannelstayon	Randallstown.
rao	row. famous Bawlmer *rao* hases.
rap	ripe. see *tamater*.
rar	raw. see *urshter*.
rarerao	railroad. see *Beeno*.

rate	right. "*Rate* cheer, *rate* nal."
rayon	round. see *spear*.
reef	wreath. see *Crissmiss*.
rench	rinse. "Affer yew finish eating crabs, iss real important ta *rench* yer hands off good."
retar	retire. "Waller's gunna *retar* nex year, Hon."
rezavore	reservoir. see *Purdybuoy, Loch Raben*.
Ricerstayon	Reisterstown.
rifmetic	see *maffmatics*.
rilliter	realtor. "Oncet he got fard ferm de SemLem, Jimmy storted as a *rilliter* fool tom."
rillity	realty. "Nal he works fer Pigtayon *Rillity*."
rilloz	realize. "Ah bet yew din *rilloz* Babe Roof yewsta be an Oryul."
rilly	really. "Nao, *rilly*, he yewsta be onna Innernashnul Lig Oryuls, but Jack Dunn sold him to Boston."
roderdenderns	rhododendrons. see *Flare Mort*.
rooer	roar. see *O's, lon*.
Roof	Ruth.
roolty	royalty.
roon	ruin. "Put it dayon afore yew *roon* it."
roont	ruined. "Nal look what yew done. Iss *roont*."
rosin	rising. "A *rosin* tod liffs awl boats."
rostrum	rest room.

rowwerskates	rollerskates. see *hosbiddle*.
rubbage	rummage.

ruff	roof. see *chimbley, airyul, hosbiddle*.
rum	room. "Buzzy, dere ain no mooer *rum* in de attic. Dose olt Playbuoys gotta gao."

S

sab	salve. "Put a dabba *sab* owen it."
sahn	sign. "Ah ain gunna *sahn* nuffn wifaout ma favver gess here."

Sairdee	Saturday. The day the front stoop gets scrubbed.
sammidges	sandwiches. Harley's (Original), Ameche's (Champ), Gino's (Giant), Polack Johnny's (Unburger).
sane	saint. see *Cafflick, muvver*.
Sandy Clouse	Santa Claus. "Happy Crissmiss ta awl en ta awl a good nate."
sanny	sandy. see *sawl*.
sanse	science. as in Murlin *Sanse* Senner.
sarn	siren. see *far, pleece*.
sarr	not sweet.
sarsage	sausage. see *brekfess*.
sarser	saucer. "Gimme a *sarser* ta kitch ma coffee in, Hon."
sawl	soil. *Cway, sanny, er uvver*.
Sawsberry	Salisbury.
scome	let's go home. "Ah'm tarred Hon, *scome*."
scooer	score. "Want chew keep *scooer* fer a wowl, Hon?"
screems	screens. see *winder*.
scullions	scallions. "No *scullions* fer me, Hon. Ah got me a date."
seccerterry	secretary. "F u cn rd ds, u cn b a *seccerterry*."
sedimenterry	sedentary.
seed	seen, saw. "Ah ain *seed* nuffn lake dat since Ah *seed* Buddy Young racing de Bawlmer Coat."
see-sol	see-saw.

seff	self.
sem	seven. see *lem*.
semdy	seventy.
semf	seventh.

7

shabe	shave. see *shorp*.
share	shower. "Sabe wooder, share a *share*."
shanny	shiny.
shaller	shallow.
Shebby	Chevy.
Shebberlay	Chevrolet.
Shicargo	Chicago.
Shirl	Cheryl.
shooer	shore. "Goan downa *shooer*..."
shooer	sure. "Ah *shooer* do miss de Coats."
shorp	sharp. see *shabe*.
shubble	shovel. see *gorden*.
Sibic Senner	De Bawlmerena.
sis	six.
sisteem	sixteen.
sisty	sixty.

6

skewl	school ...hah, prokyul, tet, seccerterry, byewdy...
skorsh	squash.
slammy	slimy. "Dese urshters er nace en *slammy*."
slod	slide. "*sloddin* booerd."

slop machine	slot machine. see *Allanic* Siddy.
smol	smile. "Gib us a *smol*, Hon."
smort	smart.
snao	snow. see *mergency*.

SNAO MERGENCY!

snoo?	What's new?
snoo few?	What's new with you?
sod	side. "Hews *sod* er yew owen?"
sodey pop	soft drink.
sollence	silence. see *quat*.
sore	sewer.
sorge	sewerage.
sorse	sauce. Harley's.

So-skyurty	Social Security.
souff	south. see *Naplis, Annarunnel*.
sparris	birds or Sparris Point. see *Beflum, dePoint*, also *plooshin, sut*.
spear	sphere. see *rayon*.

spearmint	experiment.
speck	expect. "Ah guess yew *speck* me ta clean dat up."
spensive	expensive.
sperled	spoiled. "Dese crabs smell lake dere *sperled*."
speshly	especially. see *nace*.
spicket	spigot. see *wooder*.
splanation	explanation. see *woff*.
splane	explain. see *annis*.
spoza	supposed to. see *orter*.
sprang	spring. see *gorden, faw*.
squinch	squint. see *ah*.
srimp	shrimp.
srine	shrine.

stadyum	stadium. see *moryul, O's, Coats.*
stanyard	standard.
starfame	styrofoam.
stoll	style.
stooer	store. see *grosher.*
stoonts	students.
stoop	step. see *morble.*
stort	start. see *gao.*
strang	string.
strenth	strength. "He doan nao his owen *strenth.*"
sued	suit. see *clays.*
sumair(s)	somewhere. "He leff it *sumair* ober dere. It muss be *sumairs* rate rayon cheer."
summereen	submarine.
summooer	some more. "Gimme *summooer* ub dose crab flaybered tater chips, Hon."
sumpn	something. "Yew muss fink yer really *sumpn.*"
Sunny	Sunday. see *Coats.*
sut	soot. see *dePoint.*
suvvern	southern. Hah Skewl, Murlin.
sympathy	symphony. see *Marhoff.*

T

ta	to.
tagger	de black en arnj-straped ammal in de zew.
tah	tie. "Ah can't work nao job wir Ah gotta wir nao *ta*."
tahnny	tiny.
tal, tayul	towel. "Gimme a *tal*, Hon."
Talzon	Towson. another test for new TV and radio reporters, "Toe-sun?
talzon	thousand. see *falzon, ten hunnert*. **1,000**
tamarr	tomorrow. "Ah'm gettin new bowwin shews *tamarr*."
tamater	tomato. see *mater, rap*.
Taota	Toyota.
tar	tire. see *far*.
tar arn	tire iron. Marquis of Bawlmer's rules.
tare	tower. Shot *Tare*.
tarred	tired. "If yer *tarred*, shet awf dat TB."
tarpoleon	tarpaulin. "Ah yewsta nao de guy what rowed aout de *tarpoleon* fer de Oryuls."
tate	tight.
tater	potato. see *patater*.
taw	see *draff, tare, TB* Hill.

 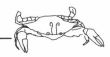
tawlet	toilet. see *fraon, snao, mergency*.
tayon	town. *Hollin, Ricers, Rannels*, Pig...
TB	TV. Pete de Part, Misser Poplowwie, Romper Rum en Miss Nancy, DoBee en DontBee, Bozo de Clayon, Dollin fer Dowwers, StuKerr, Rhea, Jerry Turner, Rolf Hertsgaard, Vince Bagli...

telebision	television. see *TB*.
tempcher	see *hut, yewmid, wevver*.
temf	tenth.

10th

ten hunnert	# 1000 one thousand. "Waller growed up in de *ten hunnert* block ub Fort Abenoo." see *falzon, talzon*.
tet	tech. "Murca's future is in hah *tet* - yew nao - Intendo, laser bums, en HDTB."
tetnology	technology.
tewel	tool. "Annis Awfser, dese ain ma burguler *tewels*."
thamometer	thermometer.
thee-ater	theater. see *moobies*.
thurpy	therapy.
tom	time. "What *tom* does de bowwin owie open?"
tootpace	toothpaste. "Doan forget en pack yer *tootpace*."
torst	tourist.
trah	try. "Mebbe dey doan look purty ta yew, but *trah* summa dese crabs. Dere well wurf it, Hon."
tret	tread. "Doan *tret* owen me."
trod	tried. "Ah *trod* ta warn yew."
trowwie	trolley. "Awl Bawlmer's ol' *trowwies* er in Eassern Yurp."
tugivver	together. "De two ub yews *tugivver* ain got de brains yew was borned wif."
turble	lake *harble* but not sao bad.
twenny	twenty. # 20

71

twiced	defnitly mooer den oncet.
twon	twine. see *strang*.

U

ub	of. "...Ore de lan *ub* de free en de haome *ub* de brabe."
umpar	umpire or empire. see *kiw*, also *Umpar* State Building.
unbenounced	unbeknownst.
unnerstean	understand. "Dat torst dint *unnerstean* us, Buzzy."
urshters	oysters. Oney in munfs wif r's.
uvver	other. "Dere ain nao *uvver* fird baseman lake Brooks."

V

vampar	vampire. see *Pao, kiw*.
varse	virus.
vee-hickle	vehicle. see *core, oughtamobill*.
veggible	vegetable. see *A-rabber*.
venchully	eventually. "Wull get dere *venchully*."
vocabberlerry	vocabulary. A pareful tewel in de rate hands.
vollate	violate. see *Pleece, ordiance*.

Vollet	Violet.
vollince	violence. "Dere's too much *vollince* owen TB."
vomick	vomit. eee-yew! see *hosbiddle*.
vonnul	vinyl.
vroddy	variety. "Suzee naos a wad *vroddy* ub hair stolls."
vydock	viaduct. Orleans Street.

W

wabe	wave. see *O's*.
Waberly	Waverly. Quat nal. see *O's, gun*.

wal	wow.
Waller	Walter. *Waller's* Ort Garry.
want	why don't. "*Want* chew set a wowl, Hon?"
war	wire. see *far*.
war	why are. "*War* yew in sech a hurry?"
warn	wiring. "De lectric's good but de *warn's* bad."
warsh	wash. "*Warsh* yer face afore yew kiss yer grand muvver."
Warshnin	Washington. see *loss*.

WARSHNIN
10 MOLLS

Bawlamorons Turn Back Nal
Afore Yew Get Loss

wat, wot, wyatt	white.
waw	wall. "We bin hangin drah *waw* fer free munfs nal. Hal come yew axed?"
wayasec	wait a second. "*Wayasec* Hon, Ah'm almos frew."
waymint	wait a minute. "*Waymint* Hon. Ah'll be rate dere."
weeb	weave. Misser Ray's Hair *Weeb*.

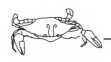 
wennup	no longer functional. see *lectric, injin*.
Wessern	Western. Hah Skewl, Murlin, Oughtao.
Wessminister	Westminster.
wevver	weather. see *yewmid*.
whatfer	all purpose interrogative. see *hal come*.
wif	with. "Hey Hon, war yew goan *wif* dat beer?"
winder	window. see *screems*.
winner	winter. see *snao, mergency*.
wir	we're, where, wear. "*Wir* not goan anyplace *wir* dey *wir* Yankee hats."
woan	won't. see *doan*.
woff	wife. "Hey Buzzy, yer *woff's* owen de phane. Er yew here?"
wooden	wouldn't. "*Wooden* it be nace?"
wooder	water. see *zink*.
wowl	while. "Iss been a *wowl*, ain't it?"
wowld	wild. "*Wowld* thang, Ah fink Ah lub yew."
wudden	wasn't. "*Wudden* de Lass Game at Moryul Stadyum sumpn?"
wull	we'll. "*Wull* meet chew at de SemLem."
wurf	worth. "What's it *wurf* ta yew?"

x-raided   x-rated. deBlock.

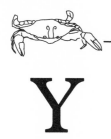 
Y

yahoo	see *ijut, maroon.*
yell	you'll. "Oltnao if *yell* lake urshters er not."
yeller	yellow.
yello	yes/hello.
yew	you. "*Yew* talk jess lake a real Bawlamoron."
yewman	human. "Ta air is *yewman*, ta forgib divon."
yewmid	humid. see *wevver.*
yewjally	usually. "De sof crabs er *yewjally* good here."
yews	you. plural, Bawlmer equivalent of "yawl."
Yurp	Europe.

Z

zackly	exactly. "What's it coss, *zackly*?"
zeeber	de ammal in de zew wif black en wot strapes.
zew	war dey keep de wowld ammals.
zink	sink. see *wooder.*
zollaphane	xylophone.

Postscript

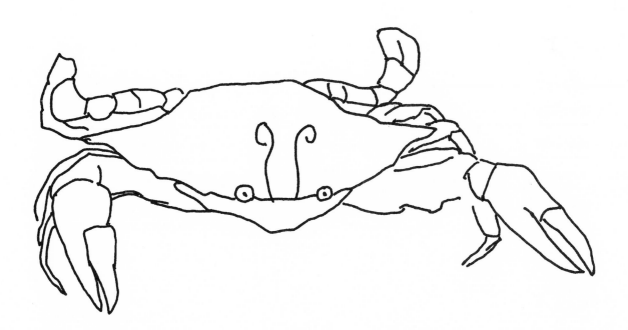

 HEY HON!

Postscript: Eulogy for a Lively Corpse

To paraphrase Mark Twain, the reports of the death of Bawlmerese have been greatly exaggerated. Sure, things are different from when my old man was a kid, but some people seem to have confused change with decline.

There is a misconception that a language is somehow unchanging and separate from its speakers. Recent contentions that Bawlmerese is a dead language are wrong. The language of my home town is merely evolving.

With each new generation some social commentator mourns the death of the "real" language - the one they used to hear. They see the shed skin of an evolving language and believe the body has evaporated when it has really just moved on.

Kids grow up, go to school, move away. The old neighborhood isn't like it used to be. The language doesn't stay the same either, but it has always been changing.

Cockney influences arrived with the first colonists. Their corruptions of the English spoken by Lords Baltimore and Calvert mingled with the accents of German immigrants to form early Bawlmerese. As wave after wave of new folks arrived from Italy, Central Europe, and West Africa, the language evolved. The twang of the West Virginia hills arrived with the Depression, adding yet another flavor to the stew.

I will admit that some of the classic Bawlmerisms of the past are gone. When was the last time you said or heard *Beeno*? For that matter, when was the last time you or anybody else actually rode on the Baltimore & Ohio Railroad? It's been out of business for a generation.

When my dad was growing up, the streets of Bawlmer were paved with *macadmium* and milk was kept in the *acebox*. Words like *Gunfer* and the *Sibic Senner* have faded too, but that's because Gunther beer is gone and the Civic Center is now the *Bawlmerena*.

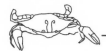 

As much as I might mourn the passing of such peculiarly Bawlmeristic terms, I am equally heartened by new ones such as *nuculer*, *starfame*, *Dizzy Whirl*, and *Intendo*.

My real faith in the vitality of Bawlmerese comes from the kids. As some wiseacre once said, it is the responsibility of each generation to infuriate its parents. My generation grew long hair and rejected most of our parents' advice until we became parents. My kids and their friends have decided to infuriate their "suburbanized" parents by speaking Bawlmerese.

It's *Hon* this and *Hon* that, and don't forget them *Ao's*. A number of kids in my son's English class recently handed in stories written in Bawlmer dialect. Whenever three or four of them get together they sound like a bunch of Buzzys at the Stadium Lounge.

They are proud of Bawlmerese. Having grown up in and around a town with a unique sound, they relish their natural skills at Upper Chesapeake Adenoidal. It's like showing off their crab picking talents to out-of-towners. Of course it doesn't hurt that it's fun too. Being native Bawlamorons, they are allowed to laugh at themselves.

Beyond the fun there is something special about sharing an accent. It is the feeling that you belong. Whenever I hear Senator Barbara Mikulski speaking before the United States Senate I feel proud. Whenever a Bawlmer accent slips through on the national media, my ears perk up. I love when an Orioles game is on national TV so that the whole country can hear the "*AO!*" in the national anthem.

I am sorry for those who think Bawlmerese is dying. They'll never experience the sense of shared community I get, over to Eastpoint Mall of an afternoon, listening to the comforting tones of generations of Bawlamorons. As long as the sounds of Bawlmer give us these feelings they will never die.

 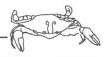

In Conclusion

If you have enjoyed this guide to Bawlmerese, please go out and visit the neighborhoods. Have a beer in a corner tavern, ride a bus, bowl a few frames - the true charm of this language can best be appreciated when heard in its natural environment.